I0605810

THE LITTLE GUIDE TO

BURBERRY

First published in 2026 by OH
An Imprint of HEADLINE PUBLISHING GROUP LIMITED

1

Disclaimer:
This book has not been licensed, approved, sponsored, or endorsed by Christian Louboutin or any rightsholder(s) in respect of this brand.

Burberry is a registerd trademark owned by Burberry Limited, London

Cataloguing in Publication Data is available from the British Library

ISBN: 978-1-03543-345-2

Compiled and written by Katie Meegan
Editorial: Shazia Fardous and Phoebe Hills
Designed and typeset in Avenir by Stephen Cary
Project manager: Russell Porter
Production: Marion Storz
Printed and bound in Dubai

MIX
Paper | Supporting responsible forestry
FSC® C104740

Headline's policy is to use papers that are natural, renewable and recyclable products and made from wood grown in well-managed forests and other controlled sources. The logging and manufacturing processes are expected to conform to the environmental regulations of the country of origin.

HEADLINE PUBLISHING GROUP LIMITED
An Hachette UK Company
Carmelite House, 50 Victoria Embankment, London EC4Y 0DZ

The authorised representative in the EEA is Hachette Ireland, 8 Castlecourt Centre, Dublin 15, D15 XTP3, Ireland (email: info@hbgi.ie)

www.headline.co.uk www.hachette.co.uk

THE LITTLE GUIDE TO

BURBERRY

STYLE TO LIVE BY

Unofficial and Unauthorized

CONTENTS

INTRODUCTION

There are very few fashion houses that can claim the longevity, innovation and quality that Burberry can. Founded by Thomas Burberry in 1856, Burberry is synonymous with one of the most interesting and versatile pieces of clothing ever invented – the trench coat. The roots of the trench coat were made possible by Thomas Burberry's ground-breaking invention in 1879 – gabardine material. The first of its kind, gabardine was a light-weight, water-resistant material used by Arctic explorers, mountain climbers and aviation pioneers.

World War One birthed the trench coat. Many of the features of the common trench coat can be traced back to its military origins – epaulettes for officers to show their rank, gun flaps to shield against recoil and D-ring belts to attach grenades. Today, the trench coat is more likely to be worn in the boardroom than on the front line, but the subliminal authority that a trench coat carries cannot be easily dismissed.

After the war, the Burberry trench soon became integrated into civilian life, becoming the go-to choice for outdoorsy men and women. The Burberry trench quickly cemented its place on the silver screen: firstly through the hard-boiled detective noir, then the subversive sexiness of the *femme fatale* who gave way to the *ingénue*, exemplified by Audrey Hepburn.

The "yuppies" of New York in the 1980s were obsessed with the Burberry trench coat – a symbol of upward mobility in a fiercely competitive capitalistic landscape. Meanwhile, across the pond, Burberry remained the preferred coat of the royal family, as well as London's fashionable sets. Today, the trench remains a staple, easily paired with anything from a formal evening dress to tailored athleisure.

Read on to learn about Burberry's extraordinary history, its most famous pieces and patterns, and those who have shaped the brand into the iconic fashion house it is today.

CHAPTER ONE

THE BIRTH OF BURBERRY

BURBERRY'S ORIGINS CAN BE TRACED TO 1856 WHEN IT WAS FOUNDED BY THOMAS BURBERRY, A HUMBLE DRAPER'S APPRENTICE FROM BASINGSTOKE, ENGLAND.

HIS INVENTIVENESS AND CREATIVITY WOULD CREATE A BRAND THAT WOULD CHANGE THE FACE OF OUTERWEAR FOREVER.

Thomas Burberry was born on 27 August, 1835, near Dorking in Surrey.

The son of a farmer, he was apprentice to a local draper before opening his own shop in Basingstoke in 1856 – at the age of just twenty-one.

“There is no such thing as bad weather, just bad clothing.”

Alfred Wainwright

Renowned British fellwalker and guidebook author. This was the basis of Thomas Burberry's ideas for developing outerwear that was suitable for all weather conditions.

Thomas Burberry recognized a market need for comfortable, lightweight outerwear. The heavy garments designed to combat British weather were restrictive and unpleasant to wear.

Thus came his vision: to create a breathable fabric that would transform outerwear into clothing that was comfortable and allowed people to move freely, while still protecting them from harsh weather.

Thomas Burberry quickly sealed a reputation among the middle and upper classes for providing high-quality outdoor wear.

The Burberry factory soon became an important employer in the then-small town of Basingstoke, with its workforce increasing from 70 people in 1871 to 200 by 1881.

Burberry's interest in creating a superior type of waterproof was sparked by a conversation he had with a doctor… the doctor expressed his opinion that the ideal waterproof was one which would protect the wearer from the wind and rain, but would also allow air to reach the body.

”

Caroline Young

Fashion writer and historian on a chance conversation with a doctor that lead to Burberry's most innovative breakthrough, *The Story of the Burberry Trench* by Caroline Young, 2024

Thomas Burberry was a very bold gentleman. He took risks.

”

Riccardo Tisci

Creative Director of Burberry from 2018 to 2022, thetimes.com, 7 March 2023

In 1879, Thomas Burberry invented gabardine, a water-resistant fabric made by waterproofing the individual strands of material before tightly weaving the fibres into a twill pattern.

Burberry was inspired by the gabardina of the Middle Ages – loose, long garments worn as outer garments by beggars, which is the origin of the name gabardine.

Until then [the invention of gabardine], waterproof macs were made of rubberised cotton – a heavy fabric that would cause the wearer to sweat profusely… gabardine's fibres were individually waterproofed *before* weaving, making it lightweight, comfortable and considerably less sweaty.

Natalie Hughes

On the difference between the Mackintosh coat and the Burberry coat, harpersbazaar.co.uk, 13 October 2023

Gabardine revolutionized outerwear.

By coating individual fibres with lanolin (a fatty substance derived from sheep's wool) before weaving, gabardine could be made from lighter materials, thereby avoiding the heaviness of traditional outwear, and creating lightweight, breathable garments.

Burberry patented the gabardine method in 1888, ensuring that only Burberry could make and sell clothes using this method.

Once the patent expired, the gabardine method became a fashion staple and is still widely used today – not only for outwear, but suits, sportswear and uniforms too.

For its logo, Burberry has been represented by the Equestrian Knight Design since 1901.

The winner of a logo design competition, the knight is said to encapsulate honour with a banner that reads "prorsum" – the Latin word for "forwards."

Today, Burberry Prorsum is the name given to the house's high-end fashion and accessory line.

PRORSUM

In 1891, Thomas Burberry opened his first shop at 30 Haymarket in London, UK.

Burberry then opened its first international store in 1909, at 8-10 Boulevard Malesherbes in Paris, France.

Burberry only opened its New York flagship store in 1978, but this was just the beginning – the brand now boasts over 50 stores in the United States.

In 1912, the iconic London Burberry headquarters were built at 18-22 Haymarket. Designed by architect Walter Cave, Burberry moved in the following year, and the building remained the company's London home for nearly 100 years.

Despite Burberry moving to a new London headquarters at Horseferry House in 2009, you can still find the brand name engraved in Burberry's former Haymarket home.

CHAPTER TWO

THE TIMELESS TRENCH

ONCE ASSOCIATED WITH THE BLOODSHED OF WORLD WAR I, THE BURBERRY TRENCH COAT IS NOW A FIRM FASHION STAPLE.

THE TIMELESS TRENCH IS THE EPITOME OF BRITISH ELEGANCE, AND WHILE NOW ADOPTED BY BRANDS ACROSS THE WORLD, BURBERRY'S TRENCH REMAINS THE HIGHEST RANKING.

IN THE WORDS OF *VOGUE*, NOBODY CAN CRAFT A TRENCH COAT QUITE LIKE THE HOUSE OF BURBERRY...

Gabardine didn't only transform fashionistas' wardrobes, but explorers' too. In 1893 the Norwegian polar explorer, zoologist and Noel Peace Prize laureate, Dr Fridtjof Nansen, wore Burberry's innovative fabric in the Arctic Circle.

While Nansen was the first recorded polar explorer to do so, he certainly wasn't the last – celebrated British explorer Sir Ernest Shakleton wore Burberry gabardine on three different expeditions.

For sledge journeys, where one has to save weight, and to work in loose, easy garments, I must unhesitatingly recommend Burberry.

”

Roald Amundsen

Norwegian explorer and the first man to reach the South Pole, newyorker.com, 7 September 2009.

Following his invention of gabardine, Burberry went on to create the Tielocken coat – the trench coat's predecessor. Burberry's idea for the jacket was to blend the formal trapping of a topcoat with the protective nature of outerwear.

Popular among Army officers in the Boer War, the Tielocken was then updated with D-rings, chest flaps and epaulettes to become the iconic trench coat we know and love today.

The appeal of the Burberry trench has to be largely due to its adaptability.

”

Miranda Holder

Reflecting on the enduring popularity of the trench coat, TheIndustry.fashion, 11 September 2023

The first Burberry coats were worn by officers during the Boer War. However, it was during World War I that they truly gained prominence.

Originally called the "trench warm," only officers of the higher ranks were allowed to wear the Burberry coats, cementing their status as symbols of prestige, even during the worst of conflicts.

The trench coat's military origins can still be seen today in its unique design. The epaulettes were used to denote rank, while the storm flaps at the shoulder channelled rain away from the wearer and also protected against rifle recoil.

The optional belt D-rings were used for hanging grenades and ammunition.

After World War I, the trench coat was re-integrated into civilian life, quickly becoming a must-have status symbol for the middle and upper classes, hunters and explorers, dare devils and day-trippers.

Said the Queen to Sir Walter,
"I vow If the road's wet,
I'll kick up a row."
Said Raleigh, "Well, Liz,
I don't mind if it is,
I carry a 'Burberry' now!"

An early twentieth-century limerick printed in *Morning Post* reflects the national love of Burberry, newyorker.com, 7 September 2009

Made in the Castleford Burberry factory in West Yorkshire, each Burberry trench coat is made up of 80 individual pieces.

The process of assembling the coat amounts to 120 individual steps carried out by the factory's expert tailors.

Each traditional Burberry trench coat is made of gabardine, and the tailors also stitch the pieces together with water-resistant thread.

The process is intricate and time consuming: the collar alone requires over 180 hand-sewn stitches, a method that takes one year for a specialist tailor to learn.

“During the war I crashed into the Channel wearing a Burberry trench coat, and had to discard it. It was returned to me a week later, having been at sea for five days. I have worn it ever since, and it is still going strong.”

A 1919 testimonial from an officer in the Royal Air Force,
The Story of the Burberry Trench, Caroline Young, 2024

The key design elements include its double-breasted front, shoulder epaulettes, beige colour, belted waist, buckled cuffs, storm flap, and a checked lining that the brand has become synonymous with.

”

Alexandra Wood

Savile Row tailor, as seen on TheIndustry.fashion, 11 September 2023

Component Parts of a Trench Coat:

- Front panel, including five rows of double-breasted buttons
- A storm flap, originally known as a gun flap and used to cushion against gun recall, to redirect rainwater away from the wearer's shoulders
- Epaulette shoulder detail, originally used to show a military officer's rank
- A "pork chop" or throat latch which can be buttoned at the neck to protect against wind and rain

- D-rings looped on to the belt, originally designed for holding ammunition, now a trench staple
- A handstitched collar
- Adjustable wrist straps
- The Burberry label, stitched into the inner lining
- Signature Burberry lining, common designs being the Haymarket and Nova checks, or a repeated monogram

By the 1920s, the trench was a ubiquitous fashion object in civilian life, but still carried the dust of the battlefield as veterans clung to their hardy outerwear.

This tantalizing link to life on the margins made the trench coat the ideal companion for a key figure in inter-war cinema – the film noir detective.

“

[The trench coat] conveyed war-weariness and dislocation; neither heroes, nor cowards, ghostly figures dressed in the dark mantle [who] were in search of a place in this world.

”

Jane Tynan

Fashion writer, *Trench Coat: Object Lessons*, 2022

“

Maybe the Burberry woman is undefinable! I think it’s less about what she looks like and more about attitude.

”

Edie Campbell

As seen on vogue.co.uk, 6 June 2012

Thomas Burberry retired from his business in 1917 before passing its legacy on to his two sons and four daughters. He died in 1926 at the age of 90.

Burberry remained a family-owned company until 1955, when descendants of Thomas Burberry sold it to the British retailing and manufacturing conglomerate Great Universal Stores (GUS).

Its origins lend the coat a certain air of authority and it has been much employed in film and fiction… lending it an unmistakable air of cool.

”

Robert Leach

Fashion historian, on how the origins of the trench coat lent itself to cinema, *The Fashion Resource Book: Research for Design*, 2012

By the '20s the trench coat had hit the streets, so to speak, as soldiers came off the front lines bringing their favorite coat with them. The trench's prominent details made it a choice for the boldly-dressed man, but it wasn't until mid-century that the coat reached iconic status on the silver screen.

”

Jack Gallagher

Fashion writer, gq.com, 24 April 2021

CHAPTER THREE

ADVENTURE & ACTING

FEW BRANDS CAN BOAST ADMIRERS AS VARIED AS BURBERRY.

THE UNIQUELY BURBERRY APPROACH APPEALS TO ALL: MAKING COMORTABLE CLOTHING CHIC (AND VICE VERSA).

FROM ADVENTURERS AND ROYALS TO FILM STARS AND MUSICIANS, THE ALLURE OF BURBERRY IS TRULY IRRESISTIBLE.

Back on land, the Burberry coat continued to be a firm favourite of both the country and city elite.

The house soon extended its range into tailored woollen suits for women, and even began to gain in popularity across the Atlantic Ocean with high-end New York department stores.

All these endeavors combined a distinct brand of heroic masculinity with nationalism and a heroic sense of Britishness. It's unsurprising that Burberry's earlier years are rooted in the British Empire and a colonial view of the world.

”

Professor Andrew Groves

Director of the Winchester Menswear Archive, harpersbazaar.com
20 February 2023

As the originator of the trench, Burberry has been a silent influence in countless films, providing straight-from-the-runway pieces and serving to inspire looks worn during now-iconic scenes.

”

Janelle Okwodu

Fashion writer, "Here's Looking at You, Burberry! The Trenchcoat's Greatest Moments on Film", vogue.com, 21 February 2016

By the 1920s, with some distance from the horrors of the global conflict, the trench coat was now synonymous with the romantic notion of the worn-out veteran, wearing his wartime clothing in civilian life.

Caroline Young

Fashion writer, *The Story of the Burberry Trench*, 2024

The versatility of the trench continued to appeal to the outdoorsy – from casual hikers right through to the most extreme of adventurers.

From early polar explorers to the first aviators, Burberry kitted out pioneers and those brave enough to step foot into the unknown.

Wearing Burberry gabardine jackets and hobnail boots, and carrying a rudimentary oxygen supply, their gear was a far cry from the hi-tech protective clothing worn by modern mountaineers.

Jon Kelly

On George Mallory and Andrew "Sandy" Irvine's attempt to climb Mount Everest in 1924, bbc.com, 3 October 2011

From trenches to the skies, a Burberry design became an essential part of any explorer's uniform.

In 1937, Burberry sponsored a world record attempt by pilots Betty Kirby-Green and A.E. Clouston.

In a beige-painted plane that was named "The Burberry" the pair flew from Croydon to Cape Town, beating all previously held records.

Burberry is a story of creativity, exploration, innovation and community – all of which continue to be at the heart of the brand.

Carly Eck

Burberry archive and brand curator, harpersbazaar.com, 23 March 2023

It was not only men conquering the outdoors that favoured Burberry, the first women to embrace adventures and record-breaking also proved to be steadfast fans of Burberry, and their outerwear was comprised of the very same light-weight and element-resistant gabardine.

They are made long enough to cover our knees… and are not always blowing open. Most motorbike clothing… is very hot and stuffy in warm weather but this is not the case with Burberry, which we wear in all seasons.

”

Nancy and Betty Debenham

The famous motorcycling sisters praise of Burberry trench coats in their 1928 manual *Motorcycling for Women*.

“I consider [the Burberry trench] ideal. I could keep dry… in the severest monsoons… and appear well dressed in fine weather.”

Mildred Bruce

Avid motorcyclist, powerboat enthusiast and one of the first women to fly a light aircraft, thetimes.com, 7 March 2023

Burberry was often the first choice of clothing for record-breaking adventurers and pioneers.

In 1930, Mildred Bruce became the first woman to fly solo from the UK to Japan, the entire time wearing a reversible Burberry trench – gabardine on one side to protect from the elements and a tweed side, which could be reversed to create a tailored look for disembarking.

There is no one who exemplifies the hard-boiled detective quite like Humphrey Bogart.

Clad in a fedora and a Burberry trench coat tied at the waist, the enduring image of Bogart as a masterful anit-hero began in the 1941 production of *The Maltese Falcon* through to 1946's *The Big Sleep*.

However, it is in the war romance-adventure classic *Casablanca* (1942) that the trench coat really gets its most iconic screen moment.

In 2005, Humphrey Bogart's Burberry trench coat from *Casablanca* sold for a whopping $10,000 at an auction!

That's the power of the trench coat. It's a coat of armour born out of dirt, fashion innovation, war and Hollywood fantasy.

”

Alison Jane Reid

Fashion writer, theluminariesmagazine.com, March 2023

There is something about the Burberry trench that can make you fall in love, it's true. It has an air of mystery as well as romance. It exudes masculinity and sexiness.

From a fashion article in *The Daily News*, March 1979

Wearing a coat that was so associated with masculinity became a form of empowerment for actress and fashion icons of the 1940s and 1950s. `

Veronica Lake, Ava Gardner, Marlene Dietrich and Greta Garbo are just some of the women who began to sport the trench both on and off-screen.

"Glamour is assurance. It is a kind of knowing that you are all right in every way, mentally and physically and in appearance, and that, whatever the occasion or the situation, you are equal to it."

Marlene Dietrich

As seen on theguardian.com, 26 November 2017

After the 1940s and 1950s, there arose a new generation of silver screen queens to be clad in the Burberry trench – the ingenue.

From Catherine Deneuve in *The Umbrellas of Cherbourg* (1964) to *Breakfast at Tiffany's* (1961), a new wave of cinema injected a fresh, almost tomboyish, romantic energy into the cinematic perception of the trench coat.

“

A trench... can be a costume for an off-Broadway vixen like Marilyn Monroe in *Let's Make Love* or a hit man's armor against a cruel world as in... *Le Samouraï*. The opposite of a statement piece, the trench melds itself to the wearer, becoming whatever it needs to be at that moment.

”

Janelle Okwodu

Fashion writer, "Here's Looking at You, Burberry! The Trenchcoat's Greatest Moments on Film", vogue.com, 21 February 2016

Of course, her hair is soaked, her shoes are waterlogged and yet… miraculously… nothing is getting through that marvellous Burberry trench coat, as it is famously designed of cotton gabardine to repel water and gave birth to the global fashion house of Burberry we know today.

”

Alison Jane Reid

Fashion writer, theluminariesmagazine.com, March 2023

I dress for the image. Not for myself, not for the public, not for fashion, not for men.

”

Marlene Dietrich

An early adapter of the trench coat for women, Marlene Dietrich was known for her subversive embrace of traditionally masculine silhouettes – yet still oozed sex appeal

The trench became so entwined with the image of the detective that it eventually lent itself to parody, becoming a comic prop to Peter Sellers' Inspector Clouseau in *The Pink Panther* (1963).

However, there was another key figure of film noir and the post-war silver screen that was also synonymous with the trench coat – the *femme fatale*.

A woman's dress should be like a barbed-wire fence: serving its purpose without obstructing the view.

”

Sophia Loren

While sporting a Burberry trench in 1958's *The Key*, using the coat as a symbol of strength and survival, people.com, 20 September 2014

The iconic Burberry trench coat, with military heritage and timeless design, is a Yuppie staple.

Mandy Meyer

Fashion consultant, thevou.com, 2 September 2024

By 1965, one in
every five coats exported
from Britain was
a Burberry product.

Search for endings of these two films: *Kramer vs Kramer* and *Breakfast at Tiffany's*. Meryl Streep in the former and Audrey Hepburn in the latter – both wrapped up and pulled together against the world in their trench coats – will make you cry and make you want to buy one. Promise.

”

Lauren Cochrane

Fashion writer, on the vulnerable yet strong appeal of the Burberry trench, theguardian.com, 20 June 2016

To the French, Burberry is the translation of *le style anglais*. For the American, the Burberry trench coat is the accepted uniform of the Madison Avenue executive. In Japan, there are 200 Burberry shops-within-shops, and the scaled-down trench coat made in Japan under licence is a top seller.

”

Liz Smith

Writing in 1988, the fashion journalist with *The Times* shares the international appeal of the Burberry trench

Less than two decades later the Burberry trench would find a new collection of devoted fans – "yuppies".

Originating in the 1980s, the term is short for "young urban professionals" exemplified by Meryl Streep and Dustin Hoffman in the classic film *Kramer vs Kramer* (1979). For "yuppies", Burberry was the perfect brand to reflect their affluence and ambtion.

You need to get yourself a Burberry trench coat.

”

Ted Kramer

Dustin Hoffman's character in *Kramer vs Kramer* states what coat one needs to be successful

In 1983, the-then Prince Charles stepped out with Princess Diana on holiday in Nova Scotia, Canada wearing matching his-and-hers trench coats from the British brand, which has held a royal warrant from Queen Elizabeth II and Charles, who is now King Charles III.

Hikmat Mohammed

Fashion writer, on the royal fans of Burberry, wwd.com, 24 May 2025

Few things are more British than a royal in a trench.

Caroline Hallemann

Culture editor, on the British symbolism of trench coats and royalty, townandcountrymag.com, 18 October, 2020

Blending traditional love of quality with a more 80s aesthetic, a group of socialites nicknamed the "Sloane Rangers" became particularly enamoured with the Burberry trench.

An offshoot of the US "preppy" aesthetic, the Sloane Rangers were comprised of mainly upper and upper-middle class young people who lived around Kensington and Chelsea.

Sloane style in particular, once dismissed as the remit of fluffy-haired girls spending daddy's money, is enjoying a return to the limelight care of British heritage brand Burberry.

Olivia Allen

Fashion writer, on the resurgence of sloane style, vogue.com, 30 April 2025

On stage, the trench coat endured a more subversive take by musicians and performers.

Prince's purple trench raincoat, paired with stockings and ruffles broke gender norms.

Punks ironically adapted army surplus and second-hand trench coats to satirize "the man", while even singer-songwriters living a bohemian, artistic lifestyle were still partial to the trench.

I chose this fabric because it was attention-grabbing and a trench because he loved the drama and the fit. You never knew what it would reveal when it blew open.

”

Louis Wells

Prince's costume designer in 2019, *The Ten: The Stories Behind the Fashion Classics*, 2021

"

It's the only coat I've got.

"

Prince

His tongue-in-cheek reply concerning his famous purple trench raincoat to an *NME* reporter in 1981

"

[The trench coat] combined with black bikini briefs, stockings and a neckerchief, Prince blurred conventional codes of race, gender and sexuality. With this controversial uniform Prince strutted onstage, intimidating and arousing crowds through his fusion of funk, new wave, punk, R&B and rock.

"

Casci Ritchie

Fashion writer, dismantlemag.com, 10 September 2018

As the trench became the symbol of the yuppie, it was also worn, perhaps with a dash of irony, by those who were anything but. Sid Vicious wore a trench coat, as did Pattie Smith.

”

Lauren Cochrane

Fashion writer, on the multifacted nature of the trench coat, *The Ten: The Stories Behind the Fashion Classics*, 2021

Beneath the measured exterior – beneath that stark, utilitarian uniform – was something else, intoxicating and violent, waiting to escape.

”

Jack Moss

Features writier, on the Joy Division frontman Ian Curtis who wore the clothes of his previous life as a civil servant, anothermanmag.com, 12 August 2019

“

I had a good raincoat then, a Burberry I got in London in 1959. Elizabeth thought I looked like a spider in it… It hung more heroically when I took out the lining, and achieved glory when the frayed sleeves were repaired with a little leather…

I knew how to dress in those days. It was stolen from Marianne's loft in New York sometime during the early 70s. I wasn't wearing it very much toward the end.

”

Leonard Cohen

From Cohen's liner notes written in 1976 accompanying the song "Famous Blue Raincoat", vogue.com, 11 November 2016

Bailey has a spiel about the trench coat and, by extension, the Burberry brand: it's for the young, it's for the old, it's for the country, it's for the city, it's timeless, it's ageless, it's been worn by everyone from Princess Margaret to Sid Vicious.

Lauren Collins

Writer, on the ubiquity of the Burberry trench, newyorker.com
7 September 2009

This Coat Never Goes Out of Style but Really We Mean Never.

A 2017 *Racked* headline, *The Ten: The Stories Behind the Fashion Classics*, 2021

CHAPTER FOUR

THE ICONIC CHECK

THERE ARE FEW PATTERNS OR LOGOS AS DISTINCTIVE AS THE BURBERRY CHECK.

ORIGINALLY USED AS TRENCH COAT LINING, THE PRINT EVENTUALLY TOOK ON A LIFE OF ITS OWN IN THE FORM OF SCARVES AND OTHER ACCESSORIES.

“

The Burberry check – a tartan design first used as a fabric lining in the brand’s raincoats in the 1920s – has long served as a visual barometer of changing tastes.

”

Laura Hawkins

Fashion journalist, vogue.co.uk, 1 June 2023

While fresh designs and takes on the check are common today, there are four "traditional" Burberry checks:

- House check
- Nova check
- Haymarket check
- Vintage check

House check

The House check is the most famous of the Burberry checks: a recognizable tan background with intersecting black and red stripes.

The design represents Burberry's heritage, evoking a sense of tradition and sophistication. Featured on many Burberry bags, this check is a favourite among Burberry enthusiasts and those seeking a timeless, elegant aesthetic.

Nova check

The Nova check is Burberry's iconic diagonal check, featuring thinner lines to create a more modern, urban pattern. The Nova check soared in popularity in the 2000s, and is commonly featured on knitwear, bags and other accessories.

Its current yet classic feel makes it a popular choice for those seeking a modern, minimalist design.

Haymarket check

The Haymarket check incorporates the equestrian knight logo into the pattern: a bold reinterpretation of the Burberry check design.

The pattern is larger in scale, ensuring that any item featuring the Haymarket check is undeniably a statement piece. This check is a playful combination of tradition and contemporary design.

B
RORSUM
B

Vintage check

The Vintage check is a modern take on the classic House check, encompassing the tradition and heritage that defines the brand.

While the check pattern is made bolder and larger, the colours are rendered softer in this check to create a muted, worn-in feel. This check is guaranteed to evoke nostalgia in whichever piece it accompanies.

The now-iconic check previously was only used to line Burberry's clothes, until in 1967, a buyer for Burberry's Paris store had a flash of inspiration.

While preparing for a presentation for the British ambassador, Jacqueline Dilemman removed the check lining from a coat to create an umbrella cover and wrap luggage. This was the birth of Burberry's check accessories.

From the 1960s onwards,
the Burberry check
has covered accessories
from hats, umbrellas and
keychains to even
prams and dog collars.

“

The pattern soon filtered down to the high streets and eventually the football terraces – it remains one of the most copied counterfeit designs today.

”

Miranda Holder

Celebrity stylist, commenting on the mass-market adoption and overexposure of the Burberry check, TheIndustry.fashion, 11 September 2023

The red strikethrough of the beige, white and grey Burberry check was worn by the Queen and tabloid favourite Danniella Westbrook alike.

Laura Hawkin

Fashion journalist, vogue.co.uk, 1 June 2023

By the early 2000s, the Burberry check became beloved of a new sub-section of British celebrity – the WAG (wives and girlfriends of soccer players).

Often fodder for the tabloids and paparazzi, these women who found themselves suddenly in the spotlight thanks to their partners' careers were sometimes mocked for their love of designer clothing or overt displays of wealth.

I'm not going to get into labels like WAG, because it's derogatory, and maybe I'm part of that culture, because I came from a working-class background in Yorkshire and now I eat at the Wolseley.

Christopher Bailey

Former Creative Director of Burberry, speaking to *The New Yorker* about the brands association with WAGs, 7 September 2009

“

We were selling products such as dog cover-ups and leashes. One of our highest-profile stores, on Bond Street in London, had a whole section of kilts. There's nothing wrong with any of those products individually… but not much of it was exclusive or compelling.

”

Angela Ahrendts

Former CEO of Burberry, who was brought in to streamline the brands offerings, including a reduction in the availability of check-covered accessories, hbr.org, February 2013

The Burberry check became one of the most copied and counterfeited designs in the world.

This cultural perception of Burberry, was cemented by the appearance of soap star and tabloid-frequenter Danniella Westbrook appearing in paparazzi pictures clad head to toe in Nova check.

In luxury, ubiquity will kill you – it means you're not really luxury anymore.

Angela Ahrendts

Former CEO of Burberry, hbr.org, February 2013

I think that probably a lot of it was counterfeit.

Christopher Bailey

Former Creative Director of Burberry, speaking to *The New Yorker*, on the proliferation of Burberry check amongst football fans, 7 September 2009

Burberry, overseen by creative director Christopher Bailey at the time, even began to limit production of its most distinctive print.

Laura Hawkins

Fashion journalist, on the limiting of the check pattern in the early 2000s, triggered by unflattering public relations between the brand and instances of football hooliganism, vogue.co.uk, 1 June 2023

Throughout the 2010s, Burberry streamlined their business, moving away from the emphasis on check-covered accessories and back to their roots – high-quality and luxury outdoor wear.

Eventually, creative director Christopher Bailey returned to the Burberry check, even designing a pride-themed rainbow print for charity in 2018.

People keep saying to me it's a plaid, and I'm like, 'No, it's a *check*!'

”

Christopher Bailey

Former Creative Director of Burberry, speaking to *The New Yorker*, 7 September 2009

However, it was Riccardo Tisci who reintroduced the check pattern to the high fashion world.

He designed a Burberry bodysuit and cape for Beyonce's *On the Run II* Tour and decked out Billie Eilish with a head-to-toe red carpet Burberry look (including a checked balaclava) for the 2020 Brit Awards.

Nova Check tartan is to Burberry what the double C is to Chanel: an instantly recognizable brand signifier.

”

Gregk Foley

Fashion journalist, sleek-mag.com, 20 September 2017

Recent celebrities to sport Burberry check variations on the red carpet include Brooklyn Beckham, Barry Keoghan, Kate Moss and Rihanna.

With the increase of celebrity fans and catwalk outings, it's safe to say that the Burberry check is officially back "in" again.

CHAPTER FIVE

BAILEY'S BURBERRY

THE NEW MILLENNIUM ALSO MARKED A TURNING POINT FOR BURBERRY.

HOW THE HERITAGE BRAND RE-INVENTED ITSELF UNDER THE LEADERSHIP OF CHRISTOPHER BAILEY AND OTHER NOTABLE FIGURES IS NOT ONLY A STUDY IN BRAND LONGEVITY BUT ALSO OF FASHION INNOVATION AND INVENTION.

He's completely oblivious [to his talent].

Rose Marie Bravo

Former Burberry CEO, describes Bailey's humility and self-awareness, theguardian.com,16 October 2013

I started at Burberry in 2001, but before that I worked at Donna Karan and Gucci, learning the business from the inside out.

Christopher Bailey

Summarizing his early career path before Burberry, theguardian.com, 21 October 2013

I was never dreaming of being a fashion designer as a kid; I was quite shy and more interested in drawing and art.

Christopher Bailey

On his childhood interests before fashion, thenewyorker.com, 8 June 2015

The son of a carpenter and a Marks & Spencer window dresser, Bailey attended the Royal College of Art.

Hailing from West Yorkshire, Bailey rose through the ranks of Donna Karan and Gucci before joining Burberry.

Growing up in Yorkshire gave me a sense of place and identity that informs all my work.

Christopher Bailey

Reflecting on the influence of his upbringing, theguardian.com, 21 October 2013

I go to Yorkshire, it's where I'm from, my family lives there and I have a house in a tiny village near to Halifax. It's kind of where my soul is; it's a very spiritual home for me as well as a physical home.

Christopher Bailey

On his Yorkshire roots and how his childhood home influences him, andrewgroves.com, 7 June 2021

So fashion was, in a way, an accident. But this world opens you up to a lot of different avenues that interested me.

Christopher Bailey

Reflecting on his unexpected entry into fashion, as a child he preferred artistic pursuits to design, interviewmagazine.com, December 2009

At Donna Karan I learned to understand the US market, about a very big corporate environment and how you need to operate within that. At Gucci it was to have a vision and a point of view, and then stick with it, hammer it, and do it to the best of your ability.

Christopher Bailey

Reflecting on key early career lessons and how these eventually shaped his leadership approach at Burberry, andrewgroves.com, 7 June 2021

My education at Westminster was brilliant for the basics, but nothing compares to what you learn on the job.

Christopher Bailey

On the difference between academic learning and industry experience, newyorker.com, 8 June 2015

I've always been a realist and I believe university can only teach you so much. It should be a skeleton, a framework, and then you go into industry and learn how to put the meat on that skeleton.

Christopher Bailey

On the limits of university education and the importance of industry experience early on, andrewgroves.com, 7 June 2021

I am confident in my own style and my own vision.

Christopher Bailey

As seen on vogue.co.uk, July 2013

From a working class background in Yorkshire, Bailey has always been passionate about giving back to local communities.

In 2008, he helped to set up the Burberry Foundation, which supports children's programmes in underprivileged areas to foster creativity, develop life skills and encourage community engagement.

I like the idea of young people taking their sewing machines and their scissors and creating something new.

Christopher Bailey

On encouraging creativity and innovation among emerging designers, reflecting his early beginnings, vogue.co.uk, July 2013

I love fashion, I love architecture and I love image making so if I can, I would put all these three in one pot.

Christopher Bailey

On his multi-faceted creative influences – as well as being creative director he also saw Burberry's relocation and refurbishment of their London headquarters in 2011, interviewmagazine.com, December 2009

I remember designing my first coat and feeling the thrill of creating something entirely new.

Christopher Bailey

Recalling his first design achievement, theguardian.com, 21 October 2013

You never feel like you're in awe of him. He's staggeringly grounded and adaptive.

”

Sienna Miller

On Bailey's character and leadership style, vogue.com, April 2018

The early days at Burberry were about understanding heritage and respecting tradition.

Christopher Bailey

Reflecting on his initial challenges when joining Burberry, theguardian.com, 21 October 2013

Christopher Bailey can be credited for the modern re-invention of the Burberry staple – the trench coat.

Throughout his 17-year tenure, he exaggerated the trench coat's classic proportions, playing with metallic materials, studs and leather.

The craft of making clothes is what hooked me initially; the tactile nature of fabric and form.

”

Christopher Bailey

On his attraction to fashion design, evident in his innovative approach to the Burberry trench, andrewgroves.com, 7 June 2021

My first fashion show was terrifying and thrilling; it taught me resilience.

Christopher Bailey

Reflecting on his early professional challenges, newyorker.com, 8 June 2015

My vision grew stronger over the years, shaped by experience and the legacy of British design.

Christopher Bailey

On the evolution of his design perspective, vogue.co.uk, July 2013

In 2001, Bailey was key to the launch of Burberry Prorsum – the brand's luxury runway line.

The Burberry catwalk was graced by supermodels Kate Moss, Cara Delevingne and Naomi Campbell with collections marked by a commitment to elegant tailoring, embellishment and British sensibilities.

His leadership transformed Burberry into a global luxury powerhouse.

”

Nicole Phelps

Fashion writer, on Bailey's impact at Burberry, vogue.com, 22 May 2019

Fashion is storytelling; I was fascinated by the narratives that clothes can express.

Christopher Bailey

As seen on interviewmagazine.com, December 2009

Bailey also lead an accessory renaissance during his time with Burberry, revamping the brand's offerings in bags, scarves and monogrammed ponchos – a style favoured by Cara Delevingne.

Real fashion things against things that have a sense of heritage.

Christopher Bailey

Describing how he contrasts modern with historical in design, newyorker.com, 7 September 2009

"[Bailey] made Burberry fresher and more relevant and helped to make the brand have an edge, whilst remaining sympathetic to its crisp, British design aesthetic."

Alexandra Wood

Saville Row tailor, rte.ie, 11 September 2023

I think there's an expectation that all fashion companies have to be cold and austere and arrogant, and I just think there are other ways of doing things.

Christopher Bailey

On making Burberry more accessible, newyorker.com, 7 September 2009

I've always loved working with people. It's really not about ego – it's about creating something we can be really proud of.

Christopher Bailey

As seen in interviewmagazine.com, December 2009

It's amazing, with age, how fabric changes. I always like things when they feel like they've had a life before.

Christopher Bailey

Reflecting on the story and wear of well-loved clothing, newyorker.com, 7 September 2009

I live with my eyes open. I never try to force myself to be inspired. I'm not someone who feels that they have to go to a foreign country or another culture to look for inspiration.

Christopher Bailey

As seen on interviewmagazine.com, December 2009

The Bailey-era of Burberry also saw the fashion house become one of the most technology-forward brands in fashion.

They were one of the first fashion houses to embrace the new era of bloggers and social media with Burberry Stories, a crowd-sourced website of Burberry street style.

Burberry was also one of the first brands to enable online shopping, making catwalk looks available immediately after shows.

Obviously, for me, that person has got to have a beauty to them – and it's not always physical beauty. It's important that I love someone's character and that I click with it.

Christopher Bailey

On what it takes to be an iconic "Burberry Girl". As seen on interviewmagazine.com, December 2009.

Former Burberry Girls include Cara Delevingne, Suki Waterhouse, the Hadid sisters and Kate Moss's daughter Lila.

That's what I get from the archives, more than 'Oh, this is a nice detail.' Sometimes it's the spirit of things.

Christopher Bailey

On drawing inspiration from Burberry's rich history, newyorker.com, 7 September 2009

In 2017, after 17 years as the creative director of Burberry, Christopher Bailey shocked the fashion world with the announcement of his departure from Burberry.

Bailey ended his reign with a final collection celebrating LGBTQ+ communities, revealed in a colourful, rainbow-themed show – even including a rainbow version of the Burberry check.

I wanted this show to be a reflection of Burberry's past and our present and also my great excitement to see what the future holds for Burberry... the next person who has the privilege of coming... into my shoes is incredibly lucky and I know they will do wonderful things and Burberry will flourish.

”

Christopher Bailey

On his final Burberry show and leaving the fashion house, fashionnetwork.com, 17 February 2018

CHAPTER SIX

BURBERRY TODAY

THE APPOINTMENT OF RICCARDO TISCI AS CREATIVE DIRECTOR OF BURBERRY USHERED IN A NEW ERA AT BURBERRY – THE MARRIAGE BETWEEN ROMANTICISM, STREETWEAR AND ELEGANT TAILORING.

TISCI HAS SINCE PASSED THE REINS TO YORKSHIRE-BORN DANIEL LEE, WHO TOOK OVER IN 2023.

Italian Riccardo Tisci studied in Central Saint Martins before joining Givenchy.

There he rose through the ranks of the beloved French haute couture house before moving to Burberry in 2018.

A firm favourite of the A-list and fashion insiders alike, his style can be described as a fusion of gothic romanticism and edgy streetwear.

I didn't speak English when I arrived from Italy in the 1990s.

Riccardo Tisci

Recalling early language challenges when moving to London, vogue.com, 28 September 2022

I was studying art… by 17 I'd decided that I didn't want to be poor anymore.

Riccardo Tisci

Showing a keen entrepreneurial edge from a young age, anothermag.com, 21 March 2014

Hired by Burberry CEO and fellow Italian Marco Gobbetti, some critics felt that Burberry became untethered from its British roots during Tisci's creative directorship.

However, it cannot be denied that Tisci brought Burberry to the next generation of fashionistas by leaning into celebrity-driven fashion, leveraging his relationships with the likes of Kendall Jenner, Zendaya and Hailey Bieber.

I didn't want to sign because I was young, I was punk.

”

Riccardo Tisci

On his original hesitation before joining Burberry, showing the juxtaposition between his aesthetic and the perception of Burberry, vogue.co.uk, 17 September 2020

The youngest of nine children and the only boy, raised by a single mother, Tisci has maintained that women have always been his greatest influence.

In 2018, Tisci made headlines by redesigning the Burberry logo. Made in collaboration with graphic designer Peter Saville, the new "TB" (standing for Thomas Burberry) monogram was release on a selection of handbags.

This move repositioned Burberry within the contemporary affinity for logos and elements of sportswear.

In the archives, I saw the old drawings… I thought, 'That's interesting.'

Riccardo Tisci

On discovering the Burberry TB monogram in the archives, vogue.com, 22 May 2019

I wanted to open up a democratic vision for the label.

Riccardo Tisci

On making Burberry more accessible and inclusive, a vision shared by his predecessor, anothermag.com, 13 February 2019

Why not develop something that represents the beginning of this new era?

Riccardo Tisci

On relaunching Burberry's classic TB monogram, vogue.com, 22 May 2019

You need a grounding to what is real and tangible.

Riccardo Tisci

As seen on vogue.com, 31 July 2020

Key stylist motifs from Tisci's tenure at Burberry include refined tailoring and gothic femininity juxtaposed with youthful, streetwear-inspired separates.

Tisci constantly played with contrasts: delicate lace versus studded leather, bold animal prints versus clean lines, sneakers versus luxurious fabrics.

It's not only a trench and a check... there was a human behind them.

Riccardo Tisci

Former creative director of Burberry on "humanising" elements of the Burberry brand, vogue.com, 22 May 2019

With time, I want to open more the archive and show history.

”

Riccardo Tisci

Creative Director for Burberry 2018–2022, found great inspiration in the archives and drawings of Thomas Burberry, vogue.com, 22 May 2019

“[He’s] ushering in a new era.”

Avery Matera

Fashion writer on Riccardo Tisci’s rebranding of Burberry, teenvogue.com, 2 August 2018

Burberry is a very special place with a magical past and a very promising future. The chapter I was asked to write in its long story is one that I am incredibly proud of.

Riccardo Tisci

From his leaving statement in 2023, theguardian.com, 28 September 2022

After five years at Burberry, Riccardo Tisci announced his departure from the fashion house.

His successor was Yorkshire-born Daniel Lee, marking the brand's return to its British roots.

My intention is to write an iconic chapter.

Daniel Lee

On his goal of creating lasting legacy at Burberry, vogue.com, 14 December 2022

I'm from Bradford, Yorkshire, very close to Castleford, where the trench coats are manufactured, and to Keighley, where the gabardine is made… My mum actually has the trench coat that her aunt had gotten as a retirement gift.

”

Daniel Lee

On his personal connection to Burberry, vogue.com
14 December 2022

As a kid growing up, Burberry is a brand that everybody knows.

Daniel Lee

On his awareness of Burberry as a child, vogue.com, 14 December 2022

Daniel Lee was a rising star: studying at Central Saint Martins before interning in Maison Mariegla and Balenciaga.

He worked at Donna Karan and Céline before being appointed Creative Director of Bottega Veneta in 2018.

Daniel Lee made history at The Fashion Awards in 2019 when he won four of the major design awards for his work at Bottega Veneta.

Lee became the first designer to win the following four categories in a single night:

Designer of the Year

Brand of the Year (Bottega Veneta)

Accessories Designer of the Year

British Designer of the Year – Womenswear

I went to New York, then Paris and then to Milan… going back-and-forwards between those various places and coming back to London as an escape or for inspiration. It's nice to be back here and based properly.

Daniel Lee

On international experiences and the transition back to London, vogue.com, 14 December 2022

Lee's debut show for Autumn/ Winter 2023 marked his first major runway for the brand.

The collection features clean, inspired tailoring and an emphasis on local manufacturing.

All trench coats for the show were made in Burberry's Castleford factory, showcasing a deep understanding of Burberry's history as well as a commitment to the future of British design.

It's not easy. I think some things just need to be kept precious. Obviously, you can play with silhouette, with form, with volume, so that's what we've done.

Daniel Lee

On designing Burberry trench coats, wmagazine.com, 19 January 2024

I think people like us, we're never satisfied.

Daniel Lee

In conversation with author Bret Easton Ellis in 2021, interviewmagazine.com

For me, ultimately, fashion is entertainment – it's joyful.

”

Daniel Lee

As seen on wmagazine.com, 19 January 2024

Burberry is characterful, irreverent, creative and hardworking.

Daniel Lee

On his definition of British modern energy, vogue.com, 24 February 2025

Throughout his collections to date, Lee has emphasized practical luxury and craftsmanship.

His Burberry campaigns have featured grime artists, footballers and the 87-year-old actress Vanessa Redgrave.

His goal, he has often stated in interviews, it to expand the version of "Britishness" that has encapsulated Burberry for over one hundred years.

Burberry is about real life.
It's about lifestyle.

Daniel Lee

As seen on vogue.co.uk, 14 December 2022

Thomas Burberry… really was making clothes to protect people.

Daniel Lee

Creative Director of Burberry since 2022 on Thomas Burberry's ethos, vogue.com/video transcript, 7 February 2025

I like to wear clothes, I like to wear fashion, and I like it to make me feel confident that I look good. So that's the mantra that I have in mind when I'm designing. People want to look hot.

”

Daniel Lee

As seen on wmagazine.com, 19 January 2024

Inherent in every Burberry garment is freedom.

Thomas Burberry

As seen on campaignlive.co.uk, 28 October 2021